READING ABOUT

Big and Small

By Jim Pipe

Aladdin/Watts
London • Sydney

Big

Eddie is at the park. What is big?

The trees in the park are big. Is this tree as big as an elephant?

Some trees are very big. But that building is even bigger!

Small

What is small?

A mouse is small, and so is the butterfly on Eddie's head!

This bug is very small. It is tiny.
It can walk around on a leaf.

Big and small

Here are two ducks.

One is big, and one is small,

like Eddie's teddies!

Here are some leaves. Which are big and which are small?

Big or small

Sometimes Eddie feels big.

He acts like a big gorilla!

8

Sometimes Eddie feels small.

He needs help to get a drink.

Bigger and smaller

Eddie plays with a football and a tennis ball. Which is bigger?

The football
is bigger.
It is as big
as a melon!

A balloon starts off small.

But it gets bigger and bigger!

Biggest and smallest

Dogs can be big or small, just like people. Which dog is biggest and which is smallest?

The biggest dog is brown and white. It walks up to Eddie.

The smallest dog is black and white. It takes Eddie's ball!

Growing

What grows bigger?

Children grow and so do plants.
Soon this flower will be bigger
than Eddie.

Animals grow, too. One day these puppies will be as big as their mum!

Getting smaller

What gets smaller?

Eddie's ice cream gets smaller and smaller, like a melting candle.

What else gets smaller?

A jumper that shrinks in the wash gets smaller!

Near and far

What looks smaller?

Near to Eddie, the boats look big.
Far away, they look smaller.

A plane is very big close up.
In the sky it looks tiny!

Sizes

It is time to go home.

Mum's bike is too big for Eddie.

This one is too small.

Eddie's bike is just right!

Goodbye!

Here are some words about size.

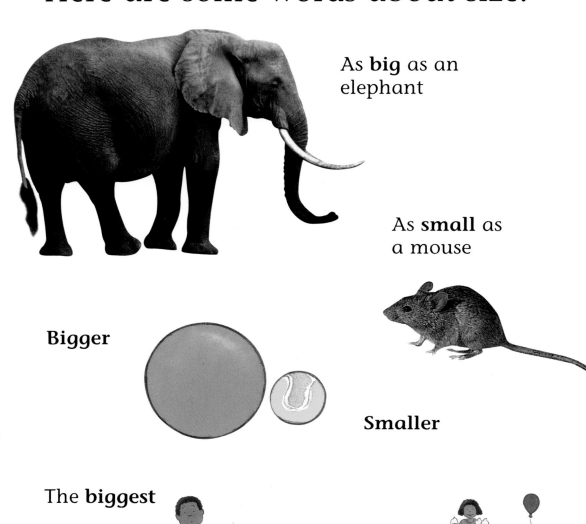

As **big** as an elephant

As **small** as a mouse

Bigger

Smaller

The **biggest**

The **smallest**

Here are some big and small things.

Bug

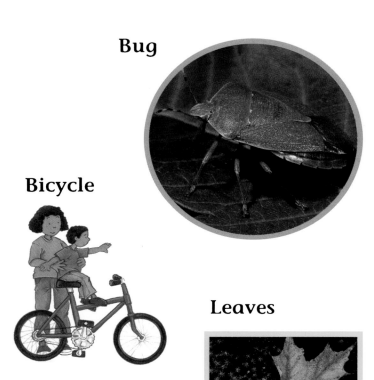

Bicycle

Leaves

Building

Flower

Can you write a story
with these words?

Do you know?

Is it big or small?

Here are three ways to find out.

Weigh it.

Measure it.

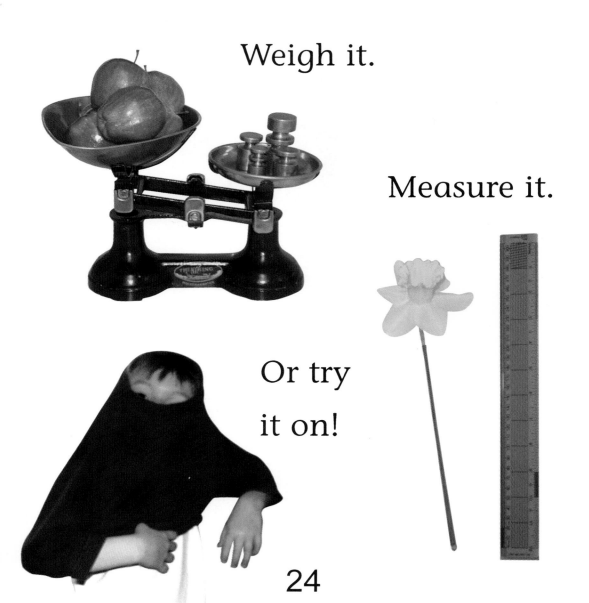

Or try
it on!

© Aladdin Books Ltd 2001

Designed and produced by
Aladdin Books Ltd
28 Percy Street
London W1P 0LD

First published in
Great Britain in 2001 by
Franklin Watts
96 Leonard Street
London EC2A 4XD

ISBN 0 7496 4120 7

A catalogue record for this
book is available from the
British Library.

Printed in Belgium
All rights reserved

Editor
Bibby Whittaker

Literacy Consultant
Rosemary Chamberlin
Westminster Institute of Education,
Oxford Brookes University

Design
Flick, Book Design and Graphics

Picture Research
Brian Hunter Smart

Illustration
Mary Lonsdale for SGA

Picture Credits
Abbreviations: t – top, m – middle,
b – bottom, r – right, l – left, c – centre.
All photographs supplied by Select
Pictures except for Cover, 7, 14tl,
18tl, 23mr – Digital Stock. 4tl, 22mr –
Jurgen & Christine Sohns/FLPA-
Images of Nature. 5tl, 6tl, 8tl, 23tr –
Corbis Royalty Free. 6b, 22tl – John
Foxx Images. 10tl, 18-19 – Stockbyte.
15 – Gerard Lacz/FLPA-Images of
Nature. 17, 24bl – Flick Killerby.

DUDLEY PUBLIC LIBRARIES

The loan of this book may be renewed if not required by other readers, by contacting the Library from which it was borrowed.

CP/494